W0075362

E-mails in English

Sander M. Schroevers

Contents

Introduction

There is no doubt that e-mail has become the dominant method of communication for people in the workplace. It is keeping us connected to our organisations and bringing us benefits like the ability to communicate over time zones. This TaschenGuide 'E-mails in English' was designed to help you integrate your electronic arsenal more efficiently into your job functions. And although anyone can technically send an e-mail, it tends to get more difficult when it deals with a foreign language. But applying what you read here will help you create a more productive union between your electronic communication and your international contacts.

The paragraphs cover a wide range of business interactions, which are organised into functional sections to provide a quick reference. The material in this TaschenGuide is written to give you the skills you need for effective business e-mails and to build your confidence in a systematic way. It is the author's hope that you will find in this book encouragement to turn writing into a rewarding activity. Wishing you every success with this,

Sander Schroevers, LL.M

An E-mail's Anatomy

This chapter focuses on the specific elements of English business e-mails, that we don't always pay attention to, but can make all the difference.

From the following pages you can learn

- how to make subject lines that work (page 5),
- which openings to use (page 8),
- and how to end an e-mail in a friendly way (page 15).

Subject Lines That Work

The subject line is one of the two most critical parts of an e-mail message. Most people (approximately 80%) make decisions on reading and responding based on the subject line and the identity of the sender, not on a first-in – first-out basis. Nevertheless a subject line seems to be one of the most neglected lines in e-mails.

How to make subject lines in English

The first step is to consider what your reader needs or wants to know from the subject line:

- Ideally, it is a summary of your message.
- Just like in journalism or direct mail: the more active and informative phrases are, the quicker they result in action. That's why mentioning essential information like who, what, when already in the subject line is advisable. Try to keep it short and simple ('k-i-s-s') and avoid vague indications like *project* or *update* etc.
- Always try to write subject lines that stimulate the reader to open your message. Should you need anything specific from the addressee, then introduce this in the subject line.
- Subject lines are also handy for people who wish to archive messages. Therefore make sure that they aren't left blank and that the subject line relates to the subject of the message. Avoid lines like: *one more thing* or *on second thoughts*, if you think that your message might be archived.

Examples

☑ Good news Schaffhausen project

☑ Action needed by 4 p.m.

☑ November 27 committee meeting

☒ Update

☒ Status report

RE: automatically inserted

Another thing is that when choosing 'Reply' most e-mail programs automatically insert 'RE:' (short for *regarding*). The same happens after choosing 'Forward' when 'FW:' is inserted. The problem is – and certainly you know this from your e-mails in German – that when a message goes back and forth several times, it might lead to unnecessary automatically expanded subject lines. This can easily result in subject lines such as: "Fw: Re: Aw: Re: Aw: Feedback on seminar Julle". You may therefore simply want to change subject lines sometimes. This also allows you to show the progression in an e-mail correspondence.

Example

I: Request for finance Hamburg project
II: Feedback requested – financing Hamburg project
III: Feedback provided – Hamburg project
IV: Hamburg project – finance request approved

Common Salutations and Openings

Salutations

Salutations or greetings can be formal or informal, depending on the situation or the relationship. And of course e-mail doesn't always follow the rules of formal business correspondence.

First name or last name?

Do bear in mind however that many English-speaking people will be quicker on first-name terms, whereas for German-speaking people it is less common to use one's first name in an e-mail message. Therefore be careful not to appear too distant in a culture which moves to first names easily because in addressing people with a more formal address, you do. And this could indicate you don't consider being friendly to your correspondent. Perhaps the reason lies in the fact that in the English language there is no difference between *Sie* and *Du*, as they both are translated with *you*.

A clear indication that it's all right to move to the first-person familiar is when a person signs her or his e-mail with the first name only. You may also wish to take the first step yourself by writing something like: *"Dear Helen (if I may)"*.

Formal or informal?

Which salutation to use may also depend on your company's e-mail policy. The table below gives an overview of the possible salutations:

Type	English	German
You do not know who you are writing to:	– Dear Sir or Madam – Dear clients – Hi everyone	Sehr geehrte Damen und Herren,
You know the person but you've never written to or met this person	– Dear Mr Smith – Dear Mrs Wade – Dear Dr Young	– Sehr geehrter Herr Müller, – Sehr geehrte Frau Reusch,
The person is a little bit closer	Dear Sophie Reusch	Liebe Frau Reusch,
The person is a close business contact or she/he has signed her or his e-mail with the first name	– Dear Sophie – Hello, Sophie * – Hi, Sophie * – Sophie – Hi, – Hello,	Liebe Sophie,
Several persons / closer contact	Hi everyone	Hallo zusammen

* Please note the extra comma!

Ms or *Mrs*? *Ms* is used more frequently in the meantime as this term does not disclose the marital status. Only if the addressee refers to herself as *Mrs*, do you assume this salutation. The English *Miss* is out of date just as is the German *Fräulein*. *Dear Sirs* or *Dear Gentlemen* also seems old fashioned nowadays.

Professions or positions in salutations

Just like it is possible in German to mention a profession or position in the opening without using a person's name, this can also be done in English. In this case, the specific word must be written with a capital. For instance as in: Dear Colleague, Dear Webmaster, etc.

Non-gendered salutations / several persons

When sending bulk e-mail invitations, try to use non-gendered salutations like *colleagues* or *friends*. *To whom it may concern* still seems to function in e-mails, though its use appears to be on the decline. Nowadays e-mail writers prefer to use salutations like: *Hi all, Hi there, Dear All, Dear Team, Dear Co-workers* and so on.

Woman or man?

With certain languages you may not always be sure whether you are writing to a man or a woman. In cases where you aren't sure, it is acceptable to write the full name in the salutation. For example: *Dear Moriko Kira* (this is a Japanese name, where *Moriko* is the female first name, and *Kira* is the family name). In Asian cultures (e.g. Japan, Korea, Vietnam, but also in Hungary) the family name comes first. Thus: *Mrs.*

Kira Moriko. Family names in Slavic languages often have masculine and feminine versions. The latter can be recognised by the female suffix, often ending with 'a' or 'e'.

No salutations?

Is it necessary to always use a salutation or greeting? Not always, although it usually is. But in back-and-forth e-mail correspondence, for instance, salutations quickly seem to be disappearing. And perhaps there is no need to identify or reinforce the parameters over and over again. The same applies for a quick answer to a short question for people who know each other well. Also e-mails among colleagues that are part of an ongoing conversation do not require a salutation or greeting.

Checklist: formal or informal salutations

1 Is the addressee outside the organisation? Then you usually need a formal salutation.

2 Is the addressee a colleague or a friend? Then you can use an informal salutation, or even begin with the person's first name.

3 Have you had previous contact? Then choose between formal and informal, depending on that contact.

4 Note how the sender addressed you. You probably want to return the same salutation.

Punctuation marks and abbreviations

Should there be a colon, a comma or no punctuation after the salutation? The right answer depends on the country you are e-mailing to.

> 🏴 no punctuation: Dear Mr Smith
> 🇺🇸 colon: Dear Mr Smith:
> In other English speaking areas a comma is used: Dear Mr Smith,

When using abbreviations there is another important difference you should pay attention to:

> Contractions in British English are generally written without a full stop, e.g. *Mr, Mrs* and *Ms* – American English usually uses a full stop however, called *period* in North America, e.g. *Mr., Mrs.* and *Ms.*
> 🏴 *Mrs / Mr*
> 🇺🇸 *Mrs. / Mr.*

Vocabulary:

colon: Doppelpunkt
punctuation: Satzzeichen
contraction: Zusammenziehung
🏴 full stop / 🇺🇸 period: Punkt

Opening sentences

Use one of the following phrases to refer to earlier contact or to give the reason why you are writing.

Formal: referring to earlier contact

- I am writing with regard to your recent e-mail.
- Referring to your request for information, …
- I'm writing with reference to order number KULIP-1.
- Further to your last e-mail, …
- I am mailing this via the 'Contact us' link on your web shop. I would like to ask you …
- Your name was given to me by …

Informal: referring to an earlier contact

- Just a quick note to say I really appreciated …
- I got your name from Dr Stampstaaf.
- Re your e-mail … (*instead of formal:* Further to your last e-mail …)

Giving the reason for writing

- Our reason for contacting you is the following: …
- *Informal:* I'm writing about …
- As discussed this morning in our telephone conversation,
- It is our pleasure to inform you of …
- As we agreed during …
- As requested in your e-mail of …
- I am writing in connection with …
- We would like to inform you about …
- We would like to draw your attention to the following: …

- Thank you for your e-mail and your interest in ...
- Thank you for the enquiry you made via our website.

> Note that in English the first phrase after the salutation always starts with a capital letter, whereas in German it starts with a small letter.

Small talk

Although the German translation for small talk is *Geplauder*, this social skill can have an important function in Anglophone cultures because small talk is not only the ability to conduct a conversation, but also a method of showing some friendliness. This naturally influences the way e-mails are written. People in North America tend to add a bit more of a personal or emotional note in their correspondence than people in German-speaking areas, although the actual choice of words depends of course on the social and professional hierarchy.

Example

Dear Thomas

I hope you had a pleasant trip and that your accommodation is fine. Although the weather can be quite cold at this time of year, I'm sure you will like the old city.

I'm writing to tell you how happy I am to hear the good news on the new business deal. My congratulations on the contract. I'm sure that it's only the beginning of our work in the Baltic market. And how are Aynur and the kids? Please give them my warmest regards.

...

Useful phrases

- I hope you had a great weekend?
- I'm writing to tell you how happy I am to hear your good news. My congratulations on your recent marriage.
- I hope you're well, and give my regards to your family.
- It would be so nice to have you over one day here in Munich.

Ending an E-mail

Closing remarks

In English e-mails it is common to include a closing remark to let readers know that they have reached the end of a message. A closing may also be used to express your gratitude, or what you expect the reader to do (e.g. answer, provide information, etc.).

Standard closing remarks

- I look forward to hearing from you soon.
- We look forward to welcoming you to Düsseldorf.
- I look forward to receiving your advice on this matter.
- We should be glad to receive this information.
- We hope we have been of help to you.
- We trust to have furnished you with all the necessary information.

Timed closing remarks

In certain situations your choice of words might be influenced by the pressure of time. The phrases below show an increasing amount of pressure:

- We hope for an early reply
- I look forward to receiving this information as soon as possible.
- I would appreciate a reply asap.
- Please deal with this matter urgently. Can I expect a reply from you by tomorrow morning, please?

Vocabulary:
increasing: wachsend
asap: schnellstens (as soon as possible)

Offering further information or service

- Should you need any further information about ... we will be happy to assist you.
- If you'd like any more details, just let us know.
- Should you have any further questions, we stand readily at your disposal.
- If we can be of service in any way?

Thanks

- Finally, we wish to express our appreciation for the cooperation we received from your company's employees during the audit.

- Thank you again for your interest in our company.
- Thank you in advance for your cooperation.

Announcing activities

- I hope I may contact you later on this matter.
- Mr/Mrs ... will contact you at an early date to explain the details.
- We'll inform you on a weekly basis about ...
- We will forward the report as soon as possible.
- We'll be glad to provide you with further details.
- We shall inform you as soon as we have the requested products in stock again.

Informal

- I'm looking forward to ... (+ ~ing).
- Please feel free to contact me.
- If you'd like more details, let me know.
- Just give me a call if you have any questions.
- Have a nice weekend.
- Speak to you soon.

Correct closing expressions

The closing or ending of an e-mail should correspond to the salutation. Informal salutation means informal closing; formal salutation means formal closing; no salutation means no closing.

Type	Salutations	Closings
You do not know who you are writing to:	– Dear Sir or Madam – Dear clients	Yours faithfully
You know the person but you've never written to or met the person:	– Dear Mr Smith – Dear Mrs Wade – Dear Dr Young	– 🇬🇧 Yours sincerely – 🇺🇸 Sincerely (yours) – 🇺🇸 Cordially yours
The person is a little bit closer:	Dear Sophie Reusch	– Best regards – With best regards
The person is a close business contact or she/he has signed her or his e-mail with the first name:	– Dear Sophie – Hello, Sophie – Hi, Sophie – Sophie – Hi, – Hello,	– Best regards – With best regards If the person is also a good personal friend: – Kind regards – Best wishes

Punctuation

As mentioned earlier there is a punctuation difference between British English and American English. But besides this, the order of the two words is also reversed:

> 🇬🇧 no punctuation: Yours sincerely
> 🇺🇸 comma: Sincerely yours,

Signatures and Disclaimers

Signatures

Make sure that your signature follows the international standards. Mention telephone and fax numbers with the appropriate country codes. Also note that the way of using spaces in numbers may differ from country to country. Sometimes city names must be translated to English. Foreign addresses can be difficult for someone who doesn't speak the language, or has a different database structure. Therefore it is best to write street names out in full without abbreviations. For the same reason it is advisable to translate the word *Postfach* to P.O. Box (an abbreviation of Post Office Box). Signatures often include a one-line description of the service the company provides. It is a subtle form of marketing.

Example

Thorsten Wächter
Muster GmbH
Musterstrasse 10 (*or* P.O. Box 123)
10100 Berlin
Germany
tel. +49-(0)30-123 4567
fax +49-(0)30-123 4589
e-mail thorsten.waechter@muster-gmbh.de
www.muster-gmbh.de

Leadership Symposium 2009 - To be held at the Muster College of Art and Design, Muster University, London.

Create an English version

Most e-mail programs allow you to make several signatures, usually by going to 'Preferences' and then into 'Signature'. This way you can make a specific English version besides your German one. You can set the preferences of the program so that the signature you use most is the standard version.

Disclaimers

A disclaimer is a statement intended to specify or delimit the rights and obligations in connection with a dispatched e-mail. Although the legal status of e-mail disclaimers is relative in some countries, you may want to use one or more of the sample texts below.

Examples

This message and any attachments are intended for the named addressee(s) only and may contain information that is privileged and/or confidential. If you receive this message in error, please delete it and immediately notify the sender. Any copying, dissemination or disclosure, either whole or partial, by a person who is not the named addressee is prohibited. Virus scanning software is used, but any liability for viruses or other devices which remain in this message or any attachments is disclaimed.

This e-mail may contain confidential and / or privileged information. Any unauthorised copying, disclosure or distribution of the material in this e-mail or of parts hereof is strictly forbidden.

For legal and security reasons the information provided in this e-mail is not legally binding. Upon request ABC GmbH would be pleased to provide you with a legally binding confirmation in written form.

> Nothing in this e-mail message amounts to a contractual or any other legal commitment on the part of ABC GmbH unless confirmed by a communication signed on behalf of ABC GmbH.

Because it can be annoying to see a long signature block repeated with back-and-forth messages, you may just want to use a hyperlink with a short phrase. This is especially helpful for people who want to print e-mail messages. To avoid the extra texts you may want to use a phrase like:

- Please visit our <u>e-mail disclaimer</u> for further details.
- For further information visit <u>www.abc.de/disclaimer</u>.

Vocabulary:
disclaimer: Ausschlussklausel
liability: Haftung, Verantwortlichkeit
disclosure: Offenbarung
commitment: Verpflichtung

Out-of-office assistant

You can create a customised message to inform people to contact someone else, or otherwise advise them on when you will be available again.

Examples

> Thank you for your message – this is an automated response. I am currently away from the office, and will return on Monday morning, 26 June. I will respond to your message upon my return. For any urgent matters during my absence, please call the office's general number (below).

Thank you for your message. I will be out of office until 25 April included. For urgent matters please contact my colleague Chiara Chessa on +39(0)4916314 or chiara@chessa.it.

E-mail Techniques: about CC and BCC

In daily life lots of people tend to send CCs or BCCs too easily. It's probably better to think a little bit about who should really get the message. A copy is best sent to people when they need the specific information for their work. But there is another disadvantage of sending too many CCs. When you send an e-mail to one person there is a big chance that you will get a reply, but if you send the message to many people the actual response rate drops to approximately five percent. If you think someone needs or doesn't need to be Cc'd on messages you can mention this as seen in the examples below.

Examples

Let me know if you still want to be Cc'd on everything, or if you'd prefer we don't clog your inbox.

I have Cc'd Maryam Salehi, who handles all translations, as well as Mr. Bagherian, the CEO.

By the way, the term BCC might be referred to differently in other languages: CCI in French or CCO in Spanish.

A Reader–friendly Approach

Most of us receive around forty e-mails a day, but many of these messages simply fail to communicate. Writing reader-friendly e-mails means thinking about your readers and their needs.

This chapter explains to you:

- when to use e-mail and when not (page 24),
- how to structure your information (page 25),
- when to write formally or informally (page 30),
- the so-called netiquette guidelines (page 33),
- how to deal with attachments (page 36).

When to Use E-mail and When Not?

Some people can get so used to e-mailing, that they also use it in situations where they simply shouldn't. Already in German daily business life, the choice between a phone call or an e-mail is substantial, all the more in an international context. And although there aren't any explicit differences between the German and Anglophone business cultures, certain southern cultures are still inclined to be more personal. As a result a phone call might be more effective than a written message there. On the other hand, a telephone call with certain Asian cultures might prove difficult at times. In such cases, an electronic message could be easier. The following general checklist can be helpful when choosing between e-mail and telephone.

Checklist: to send or not to send?

Send an e-mail	• if you need a written record to document the correspondence.
	• if your primary reason for writing is to pass on information or ask a question.
	• if you need to inform a larger group of people at once.

Don't send an e-mail	• if an e-mail seems too difficult to write.
	• if you are answering more complex e-mails.
	• if you think the content of your message is: personally sensitive, potentially embarrassing, contains confidential information or legal implications, e.g. trade secrets, job performance or hiring and firing.
	• if you need direct feed-back, brainstorming, inspiration or a serious discussion. Hold a conference call or plan a meeting instead.
	• if you have a quick question that needs an answer right away. Then make a phone call, or walk down the hall (if possible).

Structuring the Information

People who receive larger numbers of e-mails probably won't have the time to read each mail word for word. They will scan messages instead of reading them. Another thing that you should realise is that people often deal with e-mails in combination with other activities. A third point is that an inbox offers a great deal of competition. A writer of an e-mail needs to convince a reader twice: firstly to click on the message, and secondly to continue reading the content.

Writing effectively for the monitor

E-mail is usually read from a computer monitor or PDA screen. Studies have shown that people read slower on a screen by about 25%. Below are some recommendations for readability of e-mails:

- E-mail content has half the word count of a printed letter.

- Get to the point in the first sentence.

- Write in inverted pyramid style (conclusion before details).

- Use short sentences in a simple and direct style because when people are indeed scanning a message 'less is more'.

- Organize your content into logical paragraphs. Avoid long blocks of texts. Vary the length of both sentences and paragraphs. Leave extra space (between the lines) after each paragraph. Think about using short two or three-word subheadings at the beginning of paragraphs.

- Try to keep short messages within one screen, and long messages within a maximum of four screens.

- Try using bullet lists, which are easy to scan and read.

- Avoid using italics as they quickly become illegible.

- However, don't overdo it. Try to find the right balance between emphasis and readability.

Less is more

E-mails have made business correspondence more compact and most of all faster. Paragraphs in e-mail have become smaller.

- The effectiveness of e-mails is maximised by keeping them short and simple.

- That's why the language is simple, clear and direct.

- Sentences are generally short. An advantage of short sentences is that they are easier to read on-screen.

- There is more use of contractions (I've *instead of* I have, *etc.*) than in paper letters.

- If you make the reader scroll, it better be worthwhile.

Example: e-mail too long and badly structured

Dear Mrs Salehi

Following our pleasant meeting at Jamshidiyeh, I am pleased to inform you about our specific needs for the Farsi version of our on-line brochure. Firstly we will be needing adaptations of the profile page (where we could use the beautiful image from 'Keynoosh' you suggested), secondly a general introduction text concerning our publications, thirdly, idem for the workshops, and last but not least, a contact information overview. We have decided to accept your offer. If you are indeed interested in participating in this project, please e-mail us, sending your e-mail to the attention of Miss Maryam at maryam@muster-gmbh.de. She will send you all specific details. She is also the contact person should you need additional information. Thank you in advance for your cooperation in this matter.

Yours sincerely

Vocabulary:
emphasis: Nachdruck
contraction: Zusammenziehung
worthwhile: der Mühe wert

Example: e-mail short, simple, well structured

Dear Mrs Salehi

I am pleased to confirm our interest in your offer.

For the Farsi version of our website we'd need:

- a profile page,
- an introduction for the publications,
- an introduction for the workshops
- and contact information.

May I ask you to contact Miss Maryam at maryam@muster-gmbh.de for further details. I'm delighted that our meeting at Jamshidiyeh has had such results.

Yours sincerely

Techniques to make e-mails better structured

One technique is using specific linking words or expressions, indicating to the reader what the connection is between descriptions, situations or for instance, actions.

Enumerations

- First(ly)
- Second(ly)
- Third(ly)
- In the first place
- To begin with
- First of all

- Another
- Then there is
- Next
- Finally
- Last(ly)
- Last but not least

Extra remarks

If you want to add an extra argument or remark it looks nicer not only to use words like *and* or *also*, but to vary a bit. The table below offers some alternatives.

- Furthermore, …
- Additionally, …
- What is more, …
- Moreover, …
- …as well as …

- On another point, …
- In addition, …
- Besides, …
- On top of that, …

Temporal indications

- Then, …
- Later, …
- In the end, …

- Prior to this, …
- Subsequently, …
- Eventually, …

Summarising

If you want to give an overview of the points mentioned, you can indicate this to the reader by using one of the following expressions.

- To conclude, …
- To sum it up, …
- In conclusion, …
- Summarising, …
- To recap briefly, …

- All in all, …
- In other words, …
- i.e.
- That's to say, …

Miscellaneous linking words

Below are some other useful expressions for structuring the information in correspondence or reports.

- For example, ...
- For instance, ...
- e.g., ...
- As a result, ...
- For this reason, ...
- Therefore, ...
- Actually, ...
- As a matter of fact, ...

- In fact, ...
- In relation to, ...
- With reference to ...
- Regarding, ...
- In general, ...
- On the whole, ...
- Usually, ...

Vocabulary:
linking: Koppelung
prior to this: zuvor
subsequently: anschließend

Formal or Informal?

Without wanting to revert to stereotypes, it is fair to say that the British tend to be polite, whereas North Americans can be direct and optimistic in their communication. Intercultural research clearly shows that German communication can be characterised as more direct than British communication. Let's take a closer look at such different ways of expressing ourselves, and focus our attention on the differences between formal and informal, as well as the differences between direct and indirect or polite writing styles.

Informal, direct	Formal, indirect
I'm writing about ...	I am writing with regard to...
Re your e-mail, ...	Further to your last e-mail, ...
Just a quick note to arrange a day to meet. When would it suit you?	I'm writing to arrange a date for our meeting. What day would be convenient for you?
Don't forget ...	I would like to remind you that ...
So see you in Chemnitz, and do give me a call if anything changes.	I look forward to meeting you in Chemnitz. Please let me know if you need to change the arrangements.
Please send me	I'm interested in receiving
But ...; Also ...; So ...	However ...; In addition ...; Therefore ...
Shall I ... ?	Would you like me to ... ?
What about ... (+ ~ ing)?	Have you thought of ... (+ ~ ing)?
Just give me a call if you have any questions. My number is +49-12345.	Please feel free to contact me if you have any questions. My direct line is +49-12345.

Shorter words – more informal

It is also said that loan words of Latin origin sound quite formal, whereas shorter English words sound more informal. Below you can compare the alternatives (the words of English origin are in brackets).

- assistance (help),
- possess (have),
- inform (tell),
- requirements (needs),
- obtain (get),

- request (ask for),
- verify (check),
- provide (give),
- repair (fix),
- enquire (ask).

Colloquial language

E-mail can feel like face-to-face conversation, which is usually shorter and more to the point. Whether a colloquial choice of words is appropriate, has to do with the relationship with the person to whom you're writing. And as vocabulary is situational; you will need to make a judgment about the company culture and your relationship to the person with whom you're communicating. Research shows that readers of e-mails are more tolerant of a spoken-language writing style than readers of printed letters. Besides, short sentences are easier to read on-screen.

Useful phrases

- Just letting you know that I'll be arriving late.
- Could you ...? *(instead of formal:* I was wondering if you could ...)
- Just a short note about ... *(instead of formal:* I am writing in connection with)
- That's good for me. *(instead of formal:* I would like to confirm)
- I'm leaving for Shanghai, but I'll try to be there.

More personal style

Contemporary English business letters tend to be written slightly more personally then their German counterparts. You may notice this in the three examples below, where pronouns have often been used like *we*, *us* or *our*. Although the language that is used is personal, its style is less direct than speech.

Useful phrases

- We very much enjoyed meeting you in Berlin last Friday. I have now talked to Mrs Funk about our meeting and I am pleased to say …
- Following our discussion earlier this month, I regret to inform you …
- As we agreed on the phone this afternoon, I am mailing you a PDF file with …
- Please feel free to contact me if you have any questions.
- I think your idea would work really well.
- May I suggest that I call you at your convenience to discuss the matter further?

Netiquette Guidelines

By their nature, e-mail conversations tend to be rather informal and quickly typed messages. During the evolution of e-mail certain basic rules of conduct have developed, which is generally referred to as *netiquette*. Below is a selection of these guidelines:

- Unless you are using encryption, you should assume that mail is not secure. Never write in an e-mail anything you wouldn't want to write on a postcard.

- Don't send emotional messages (called *flames*) even if you are provoked. It is better to calm down first.

- It is not always permissible to forward just anything. Sometimes forwarding may be in violation of copyright laws.

Delivery and read receipts

A delivery receipt informs someone that an e-mail message was delivered to the recipient's mailbox. A second option, the so-called read receipt, informs that the message has been opened as well. The point is that the recipient has the option to decline sending read receipts, and certain e-mail programs also don't support read receipts. In daily life, you should keep in mind that asking for receipts means you are in fact freezing someone else's computer until they click on a dialogue box.

Electronic humour

When you are communicating orally, you have the advantage of vocal variety and other non-verbal communication. All of that is absent in e-mail. It is therefore important to be careful with jokes. It is better to save anecdotes for in-person gatherings. Electronic humour can be a risk especially when corresponding with other cultures because jokes don't like to travel. On the other hand, it is good to realise that in Anglophone business cultures, jokes are much more accepted and can often play an important role in creating the right professional atmosphere.

Emoticons :-)

Although e-mails often tend to be more informal, the smiley created from a colon-hyphen-close pare probably has no place in a business document. Therefore, to keep e-mails professional simply avoid all frivolous emoticons.

Gender-neutral language

With gender-neutral language one can avoid the usage of masculine pronouns. Especially in the USA and Canada many people find the usage of masculine language inaccurate or even offensive.

- Using a term like chairperson instead of chairman is a good example of acknowledging that a woman in authority will also read the e-mail in question.
- Other options for gender-neutral language are to recast sentences into plural, to use the generic pronoun *one*, to replace typical masculine words like *his* or *he* with articles (*a, an, the, this, these*, etc.), or to use plural pronouns (*they, them, their*).

Errors

Due to the nature of e-mails occasional errors (while undesirable) are not uncommon. Research has shown that readers have become much more permissive in that aspect compared to the days of paper communication. Nevertheless, errors in style, punctuation or spelling influence a professional image or, to some extent, a company's reputation. Therefore, spell-check your e-mail. Most software packages (also webmail) have an automated feature for this. Proofread e-mails, too before sending them.

How to Deal with Attachments

People don't always expect and/or welcome the information given in attachments. Besides, attachments may transmit destructive viruses and worms. It is therefore not surprising that people have become reluctant to open attachments, unless of course, they trust the sender and are informed in the message itself.

Best ways to deal with attachments

- Inform the addressee about attachments by indicating this in the subject line and/or in the beginning of the message. This is even more important since attachments aren't always indicated as such, and can only be seen after scrolling to the end of the message. This is caused by the way different software programs react on each other.

Examples

Itinerary Berlin conference - 2 files attached.
The first line might say: Two files attached.

- When an attachment is long and complex, you might consider summarising it briefly in the body of the e-mail message.

- If the purpose of a message is to simply forward an attached file, then the cover e-mail should be written very briefly, and should explain where the recipient should focus her or his attention on.

- And finally always try to give instructions to the recipient about what to do with an attachment. Do you expect the reader to file or forward it, or do you need comments?

Examples

Example: summarising the attachment:

Dear Mrs Kawashima

I am pleased to attach the new final report for Cargill Brazil. This report shows the outcome of ...

Example: indicate the addressee to forward the attachment:

Attached is the proposal for our new website. Can you forward it to all your managers?

Example: instructions on what to do with the attachment:

I've attached the draft of the final report. Thanks for using the 'track changes' feature to comment. I would specifically like to draw your attention to the section on Kyoto and Maya Bay. I will be interested in hearing your thoughts about this report's findings at our next Brazil summit.

Useful phrases

Indicate attachments

- Enclosed please find the necessary technical specifications.
- We are happy to enclose ...
- You will find particulars of ...
- A route description has been enclosed.
- For the general terms please refer to the attachment.
- Please see our prices on enclosed price list.
- Enclosed please find our latest catalogue.
- Please find enclosed some low resolution jpg images.
- Please find attached my report.
- I'm sending you our general conditions as a PDF file.

> Make it a habit to attach the file before composing the message.
> And double-check whether you attached the right file.

Instructions

- That document is stored in PDF format. You need the free Adobe Acrobat Reader to open the PDF file.
- By clicking on the hyperlink, you will be directed to the appropriate information on our website.
- Because the attached document is a bit complex, I have briefly summarised it below.
- All documents have been scanned for viruses and are compatible with Mac and PC.

Say what to do with the attachment

- I've attached the draft of the final report. Please use the 'track changes' feature in MS Word for any comments.

- Here is the design for the new Swiss brochure. We'd like to know your comments by Wednesday next week.

- I have attached the revised quarterly budget. Could you forward it to all the Düsseldorf managers?

Explaining errors when sending attachments

- I'm sorry to say that I forgot to attach the attachment in my previous mail. Here it is.

- Did you mean to send me the minutes? They weren't attached. Would you mind sending them again?

Avoiding attachments

You can avoid attachments by simply pasting the content of short files into the body of an e-mail message. This always works unless formatting is important. In this way you also save people downloading time because business travellers may have to use slow phone connections in hotels. Also users of smart phones may be charged per Mb. And they don't want to download a file for many minutes to discover there is a picture they never wanted anyway.

Vocabulary:

general terms and conditions of trade (GTCT): allgemeine Geschäftsbedingungen (AGB)

Checklist: e-mail basics

- Are the correct addressees in the To, Cc or Bcc fields?

- Think of the reader's specific information needs.

- Know which key points must be covered.

- Decide upon a good subject line.

- In the event of attachments: add these first and indicate them in the subject line or first sentences. When an attachment is complex, summarise it briefly in the body of the e-mail message. Give instructions to the recipient about what to do with an attachment.

- Announce the main point of the e-mail in the beginning.

- Write paragraphs in the 'most-important-first structure' (the so-called inverted pyramid).

- Write in an active and direct way.

- Try to use short paragraphs.

- Make use of headers and bullet points.

- Avoid jargon, specific abbreviations or technical language unknown to readers.

- Never forget that an e-mail might have unseen readers: do not send an e-mail containing confidential information or one that has legal implications.

Common Business Situations

The business situations which follow are intended to cover a wide range of interactions typical of international correspondence. The material in this chapter is intended as a sort of phrase bank and as a basis for further expansion.

In this chapter you will learn more about how to create day-to-day business e-mails:

- requesting information (page 42),
- giving enquiries (page 49),
- making appointments (page 53),
- refusing a request (page 66),
- complaints and apologies (page 69),
- making offers (page 78).

Requesting Information or Favours

E-mails in which information is requested or given are among the most common topics in inboxes. When requesting information, it is well-advised to explain things clearly. Start for instance by explaining how you obtained the addressee's contact data and then write what particular information you would like to have or are interested in.

Bear in mind that writing in a foreign language doesn't mean simply translating a text from German. Different cultures can use other ways of asking for things. As mentioned, British English formulates requests in a slightly more indirect way. For instance, by using modal auxiliaries, or using the word *please* more often. This is shown in the examples below:

Examples

Formal: to an unknown addressee
Dear Sir or Madam
During my last visit to the GDS trade fair at Messe Düsseldorf, I saw a sample of your products. Our company specialises in the manufacture of shoemaker's machines and we are looking for a reliable supplier.
May I ask you to send us full information and details of your latest models? If possible quote prices in euros please.
Yours faithfully
Silke Mertens

Formal: to a known addressee
Dear Mr Roll
I'm writing with regard to booking one of your workshops. As we are organising an in-company conference at our firm 'Innovate Consulting' this March, we'd be interested in finding

out whether you are able to give a presentation of about 45 minutes? Our focus is on creating value through a company-wide branding approach. We would be grateful for some information about your prices and availability. Should you have any further questions, do not hesitate to contact me.

Yours sincerely

Mr Pirouz Malekzadeh
Managing Director

Informal: to a colleague

Dear Pirouz

Could you send me the latest material on Mahram ketchup please? I will need it to prepare the pitch in Milan next week. I'd appreciate your help on this. Let's talk next week and see how things are going.

Best regards
Sander

Vocabulary:

modal auxiliaries: Modalverben
supplier: Lieferant
to quote: ein Angebot machen

Useful phrases

Formal: introductions

- I was interested to see your advertisement in the latest issue of 'Deutschland' magazine.
- I understand you are manufacturers of ...
- We have read about your company in the trade press.
- Mrs. Zeurpiet, we have not met; however, I would be grateful for your advice.

Formal: request for information

- I wonder if you could ... ?
- Do you think I could have ... ?
- I'd be grateful if you could ...
- I would like to know ...
- We're interested in finding out ...
- We would like to receive ...
- I wonder if you could ...
- Could you perhaps attach your current catalogue and price list as a MS Word or PDF file?
- Please send us information about your product range and prices.
- Please send full details of your prices, discounts, terms of payment and delivery times.

Informal: request for information

- Can you tell me a little more about ... ?
- Can I have ... ?
- Please could you ... ?
- Please send me ...
- Just a quick note to remind you to ...
- Your name and address were passed to me by ...
- We met last Thursday at the Leipzig Trade Fair.

Scales of politeness

British English uses different scales of politeness depending on the familiarity between people. The examples below are ascending:

- Why don't you send me the attachment?
- Send me the attachment, won't you?
- Send me the attachment, will you?
- Send me the attachment, would you?
- Won't you send me the attachment?

It isn't really possible to make such distinctions in the German language system. But when writing in English it nevertheless matters. It is therefore advised to use the polite or indirect form when you're not exactly sure about which form to use. This means that you should use *might* instead of *may*, or *could* instead of *can*. For the same reason you should be careful with translating *ich möchte* with *I want*.

Anglophone cultures don't often use a direct *no*. Therefore a phrase like: *I wonder if this is the best solution* translates best with *Nein* ...

Hotel or Conference Enquiries

Examples

Reservation: hotel and technical equipment

Dear Sir or Madam

For our company Muster GmbH from Düsseldorf, I would like to make a group booking for 10 guests. It concerns a three day meeting including accommodation. The date of arrival is Friday, June 13. We'll need two double rooms and six single rooms on a half board basis. There are no special requests.

The rooms will be paid for by the participants, and the meeting can be billed to the organiser: Muster GmbH, Düsseldorf.

For the conference, we'd like a meeting arrangement of: coffee (10:30 AM) and lunch (1:00 PM). We are looking for a medium-sized conference hall with three separate meeting rooms.

Each equipped with WLAN, whiteboards and flipcharts.

Could you please inform me on availability and prices? Thanking you in advance.

Yours faithfully

Jule Funk

Muster GmbH

Reservation: Restaurant

Dear Sir or Madam

I would like to reserve a table for four people in your non-smoking area, for tomorrow April 1st at noon.
Please make the reservation in the name of Muster GmbH from Düsseldorf. Thanking you in advance.

Yours faithfully

Jule Funk

Useful phrases

- Please reserve a single room with bath for Mr James Bond during his visit in Aachen from April 25th through May 2nd (date of departure).

- Can you offer a discount for a group of twenty-five?

- May I ask you to please quote the inclusive price?

- I attach a copy of my intended itinerary.

- Layla Kawashima will settle the bill on behalf of Cargill.

- Unfortunately I have to cancel our reservation at your hotel.

- I should like to reserve a conference hall for approximately thirty people. Is it possible to have seating in a U-shape?

- Please send us details of available conference equipment, as well as simultaneous interpretation and translation services.

- Could you inform us how much the charge per half day is for a second beamer, flip-chart and white-board?

- We would like to be picked up from the conference by coach.

Useful vocabulary

Hotel

queen-size bed 🇺🇸	1,5 m breites Bett
king-size bed 🇺🇸	2 m breites Bett
settle (the bill)	begleichen

booking request	Buchungsanfrage
executive class	Businessclass
double bed	Doppelbett, französisches Bett
double room	Doppelzimmer
single room	Einzelzimmer
half board	Halbpension
high season	Hauptsaison
low / off season	Nachsaison / Vorsaison
itinerary	Reiseroute, Wegbeschreibung
B and B, bed and breakfast	Übernachtung mit Frühstück
full board	Vollpension
no. of rooms	Zimmeranzahl
twin-bedded room	Zweibettzimer

Conference equipment

meeting room	Besprechungsraum
seating	Bestuhlung
stage	Bühne
fax service	Fax-Service
flip chart	Flip-Chart
big screen	Großbildschirm
Internet access	Internetanschluss
air conditioning	Klimaanlage
conference room	Konferenzraum
photocopier	Kopiergerät
laser pointer	Laserpointer

integrated loudspeaker	Lautsprecheranlage
microphone facilities	Mikrofonanlage
flip-over	Präsentationsmappe
lectern	Rednerpult
reach 25 m.	Reichweite 25 m
rows	Reihen
wireless presenter	schnurlose Computerfern-bedienung
secretarial support	Sekretariatsarbeiten
room dividers	Stellwände
meeting and accommoda-tion as flat rate	Tagung und Übernachtung als Pauschale
U-shape	U-form
dimming	Verdunkelung
video conference	Videokonferenz
whiteboard	Weißwandtafel
wireless local area net-work, WLAN	W-Lan

Giving Enquiries

FYI: for your information

One of the most commonly sent e-mails is the FYI. This acronym stands for *for your information*. FYI is commonly used in e-mail or memo messages to flag the message as an informational message that does not require a response. This is typically indicated in the subject line: "FYI: annual sales meeting". Sending people an e-mail without informing them you are actually sending it as an FYI might trick them into opening a mail, they didn't want to open as generally an FYI doesn't require someone's immediate attention. Because busy readers might not always read all the subject lines, it is also recommendable to repeat the FYI again in the first line of the body of the text.

Useful phrases

- For your information ...
- This is to inform you...
- Just so you know...
- I wanted to let you know that...
- This is just to tell you...
- For your files I attach ...

Answering requests

The phrases below offer content for those e-mails in which information is given based upon e-mail requests.

Examples

Formal

Dear Sir or Madam

Muster GmbH from Linz in Austria, is seeking bids for the production of several trade fair stands. May I ask you to send us your bid if you are interested?

Detailed specifications are attached. Also please note that

Muster GmbH doesn't wish to work with products that are in anyway associated with environmental hazards in the production, manufacturing or maintenance of materials.

The deadline for bids is June 26, 2011.

Feel free to contact me should you need more information.

Yours faithfully

Less formal

Dear Mr Sanchez

I was wondering if I could ask you something regarding the new product development analyst. I believe you have known him for some time and I would be grateful for any information you could give us. This will of course be treated with strictest confidence. Thank you in advance for your help in this matter.

Yours sincerely

Informal

Hi Betty,

I wanted to get the June 26 business unit notes to you as soon as possible. Please get back to me if there's any information that I can supply.

Regards

Useful phrases

Formal: enterprise and product information

- Thank you for your e-mail of 14 July enquiring about ...
- Your enquiry/query concerning our products ...
- You will note that our ... is on special offer.
- We are also happy to send you full details of our prices, discounts, terms of payment and delivery times.

Informal: enterprise and product information

- John, it's been a while since we have spoken. I'm attaching a document that gives you full details of ...
- I took the liberty to attach a list of some of our clients, which you will see include ...
- I understand that you are looking for ...
- In reply to your e-mail, here ...
- Allow us to draw your special attention to ...
- Our products are carefully tested to ensure quality.
- All our products carry a one-year guarantee.
- Of course we replace all defective parts free of charge.

Formal: more time needed

- We are behind with production.
- Because of problems with our supplier ...
- We therefore cannot guarantee delivery by June 26.
- We offer you our sincere apologies for this.
- We shall do our utmost to ...

Informal: more time needed

- I might need some more time after all.
- I'm sorry to inform you that we will not make the deadline. But we're doing everything we can to sort it out.
- I hope you will understand my position.
- I'll be in touch again soon with more details.

Change of Address

These days, more and more changes of address come by way of e-mail. When informing foreign relations, always try formatting address information according to international standards. By the way, the so-called *Landeskürzel* (e.g. D) should no longer be used.

Useful phrases

- Change of address notification: ...
- Our head office has moved to Hanover.
- We have now opened a new branch in Vienna.
- Our address has changed and is now as follows: ...
- May we ask you to please forward any correspondence to our new address?
- Change of address: as of July 1: ...
- Change of address as of May 2nd 2009: Devon House, Devon Centre, Manchester, M4 5KC.
- Our telephone numbers remain unchanged.
- Our telephone number now is: ...

Appointments

Making appointments for meetings, teleconferences or lunches are the order of the day. In general such messages can be brief, but make sure that you don't cancel appointments too abruptly. As already mentioned, all too direct communication might be misunderstood.

Examples

Informal
Dear Sara Lou,
Could we meet in the next few days? I'm open this Thursday and Friday for lunch or in the afternoons.
Cheers,
Sander

Refusing

Sorry Sander, I'm not available then. I've got an offsite client meeting. How about next week? Bisoux, Sara Lou

More formal

Dear team managers

I'm setting up a meeting at 10 a.m. on Nov. 27, 2009, together with the Marketing Department from head office. It's to review and evaluate the performance of the brand against competitors. Please let me know if you will be able to attend as soon as possible, so I can circulate the agenda.

Best regards
Martin Saunders

Refusing

Dear Martin

Thank you for your kind invitation. Unfortunately, I have another appointment on that day. But please let me know how it went.

Best regards
Sara

Useful phrases

To ask for an appointment

- I'm writing to arrange a time for our meeting. Could we meet on Friday, June 26, in the afternoon at 3 p.m.?
- Would be very pleased if you could come to a meeting here on 1 April.
- The meeting will last all morning and will have an informal agenda.
- Your presence at the meeting will be most useful.
- Please everyone let me know if you will be able to attend by next Wednesday at the latest.

Confirming proposals

- Yes, I think I should be able to make next Friday morning at The Savoy.
- I'll get back to you later today to confirm our appointment.
- Just to confirm my visit to you, on Friday 13 at 10 a.m. ET (Eastern Time Zone).
- Looking forward to meeting you next week.
- Please let me know if there's anything I can prepare.

Refusing / postponing an appointment

Example: refusing an invitation (formal style)

Thank you for your kind invitation.

Unfortunately, I have another appointment on Friday. Please accept my apologies.

In the case any reports arise from the discussion on Central Europe, I would be most grateful to receive a copy. I hope we will have the opportunity to meet on another occasion in the near future.

- I'm afraid I can't manage next Friday.
- I'm not available for lunch on either day, but would 3 p.m on Friday suit you?
- I'm out of the office until 11 p.m., but any time after that would be fine.
- This is to let you know, that I will not be able to attend the meeting in Berlin.
- Please accept my sincere apologies for cancelling our appointment on such short notice.
- I had an unavoidable emergency that prevented me from keeping our appointment.

Invitations

When accepting or declining invitations, note that in English one often tends to use adjectives like: *happy*, *delighted* or *pleased*, which in German might sound somewhat exaggerated at times. Nevertheless, it is advisable to express enthusiasm or regret with slightly more emphasis.

Examples

Invitation for a conference

Muster GmbH has the pleasure to invite you to the Conference 'XYZ', organised in Lucerne on 22 May 2009, in association with ABC-AG. The conference will take place at Auditorium KKL Luzern (Zentralstrasse 9) from 9 a.m. to 5.30 p.m. The programme will be updated regularly on the website of Muster GmbH. Please complete the attached form and return to ...

Invitation for lunch

Dear Mr Haas
I would like to take this opportunity to invite you for our monthly business unit lunch at Tantris, on Johann-Fichte-Strasse 7. Friday, 13 February at 13:30 o'clock.
Your attendance will be very welcome.

Useful phrases

Inviting and RSVP

- We would very much like to invite you for a presentation given by Mrs. Maryam Salehi on May 22 in the Khajeh Nasir Hall, which starts at 11 a.m.

- It would be a pleasure to receive you at our annual trade exhibition.

- I would like to take this opportunity to invite you for our monthly sales manager meeting.

- The pleasure of your company is requested at the ...

- Would you please send an answer to our invitation as soon as possible.
- We would very much appreciate it if we could receive your decision before 26 June.
- RSVP (regrets only): presentation@muster.de

Route descriptions and other information

- We hereby attach a route description as a PDF file.
- If this information is not accurate or if you need additional information about your travel plans or information on our company, please call, e-mail or fax me directly. That way, we will receive your message in time to make the appropriate changes or additions.
- When you arrive, just ask for me at reception.
- Again, we are very honoured that you will be visiting us, and we look forward to a successful business relationship between our two companies.

Formal: accepting / declining an invitation

- May I thank the board for their kind invitation to ... on May 22 and I take great pleasure in accepting it.
- Thank you for your kind invitation. I would be delighted to attend the ...
- I'm very sorry that I will miss the meeting. Please accept my apologies.

- Mrs Funk thanks PressEasy Ltd for their kind invitation but due to a previous engagement she regrets she is unable to accept.

Informal: accepting / declining an invitation

Example: accepting an invitation

Thanks a lot for inviting me. I'd love to come to the meeting. Would it be okay to bring Silke Mertens as well? She's in charge of the whole series. I met her in Frankfurt last year.

- Thanks a lot for your kind invitation.
- Unfortunately, I have something else on my agenda on that day.
- I'd really love to come to your lecture.

Canceling an appointment

When you deem it necessary to cancel an event and inform the participants by e-mail, it is important to find the proper tone of voice and courtesy.

Example

Dear Sirs,

Due to circumstances beyond the control of Muster GmbH, the banquet unfortunately had to be cancelled. Muster GmbH apologises for any inconvenience caused.

Sincerely yours

Useful phrases

- Owing to circumstances beyond our control, we will unfortunately need to ...

- Regrettably, due to unexpected events Dr. Doğan must cancel the lecture of June 26.

- Mr Jorritsma sends his sincere apologies for his absence from the conference, and ...

Indicating date and time

While trying to arrange an appointment, pay attention to using the proper expressions concerning date and time. Take special precautions if your message will be sent internationally to prevent misunderstandings: Spell out dates, as in Germany, 02/05/09 means May 2, 2009; but in the United States this means February 5, 2009. There are more specific differences between German and English, e.g. the twelve-hour clock, page 63. In case of doubt try to double check appointments; some people ask for confirmation by e-mail or fax. Electronic agendas like MS Outlook offer practical functionalities that automatically send reminders per e-mail.

Months

January	Januar	July	Juli
February	Februar	August	August
March	März	September	September
April	April	October	Oktober
May	Mai	November	November
June	Juni	December	Dezember

Dates

🇬🇧 26 June, reads as: the twenty-sixth of June.

🇺🇸 June 26, reads as: June twenty-sixth.

🇬🇧 26th June, reads as: June, the twenty-sixth.

🇬🇧 2009, reads as: two thousand and nine.

🇺🇸 2009, reads as: two thousand nine.

Please note that years are usually pronounced in pairs: e.g. nineteen ninety-nine (1999).

Ordinal numbers

1st - first	8th - eighth (only one 't')
2nd - second	9th - ninth (no 'e')
3rd - third	10th - tenth
4th - fourth	11th - eleventh
5th - fifth	12th - twelfth ('f' not 'v')
6th - sixth	20th - twentieth
7th - seventh	21st - twenty-first etc.

Days

Monday	Montag
Tuesday	Dienstag
Wednesday	Mittwoch
Thursday	Donnerstag
Friday	Freitag
Saturday	Samstag, Sonnabend
Sunday	Sonntag

today	heute
tomorrow	morgen
yesterday	gestern
the day before yesterday	vorgestern
the day after tomorrow	übermorgen
🇬🇧 as from today	von heute an
🇺🇸 as of today	
this Thursday	diesen Donnerstag
next Tuesday	nächsten Dienstag
by Friday	bis Freitag
on Saturday	am Samstag, Sonnabend
a week on Monday	Montag in einer Woche
a week from Monday	
🇬🇧 in a fortnight's time	in vierzehn Tagen
🇺🇸 in two weeks' time	
every Monday	jeden Montag, montags
on Mondays	
in 6 days' time	in sechs Tagen
last / next month	im letzten / nächsten Monat
last week	letzte Woche

Times of the day

in the morning	morgens, am Morgen
early morning	der frühe Morgen
morning	Morgen, Vormittag
midday	Mittag
lunchtime	Mittagszeit
before lunch	vor dem Mittag

after lunch	nach dem Mittag
in the afternoon	nachmittags, am Nachmittag
afternoon	Nachmittag
late afternoon	Spätnachmittag
evening	Abend
in the evening	abends, am Abend
in the morning	am Vormittag

What time?

Perception of time may differ from culture to culture. In the UK, for instance, people tend to give each other a margin of several minutes. The Irish saying 'When God created time, he created plenty of it' is of course only a generalisation, it nevertheless indicates that punctuality might be looked upon differently from country to country.

Therefore, always plan meetings with a sufficient margin because they may start a little bit later than expected. And also don't let yourself be too much guided by what you are used to in Germany. Apparently, six out of ten American managers are late for their appointments, according to research conducted in 2006 amongst 2,700 CEOs. This "CEO's quarter of an hour's grace" also costs companies a lot of money.

at 8 (o'clock) in the morning / 8 a.m.	um 08:00 Uhr
at 8 (o'clock) in the evening / 8 p.m.	um 20:00 Uhr

till 5 (o'clock) in the evening / 5 p.m.	bis 17:00 Uhr
after three (o'clock)	nach 15:00 Uhr
before three (o'clock)	vor 15:00 Uhr
🇬🇧 as from 3 p.m. 🇺🇸 as of 3 p.m.	ab 15:00 Uhr
between three and five (o'clock)	zwischen 15 und 17 Uhr
a quarter past nine	viertel nach neun
a quarter to nine	viertel vor neun
three thirty	halb vier
🇬🇧 half eight (half past eight)	halb neun (*not*: halb acht!)
twenty-five minutes past ten	zehn Uhr fünfundzwanzig
five to twelve	fünf vor zwölf
noontime	Mittag
half an hour	eine halbe Stunde
quarter of an hour	eine Viertelstunde
three quarters of an hour	eine Dreiviertelstunde

Sending Agendas and Minutes

There are certain standard items that belong to an agenda: like a title, followed by the date, time and venue of the meeting and a list of the people who will be attending it. In English the minutes always follow the agenda exactly. Each section of the notes is identified by the number of the item on the agenda, or the heading taken from the agenda. Below are some useful hints for making summaries.

Checklist: summary of a meeting

- **Include the date**: avoid vague descriptions like *yesterday* or *last week's meeting.*

- **List the participants**: as members of a department change from time to time, it is better to list people by name.

- **Indicate action points** to the discussed topics. Also designate responsibility, mention the possible deadline and describe each action. This ensures the action and serves as a record.

Examples

Agenda

Muster GmbH Management Team Meeting

Tues. Nov. 27, 2012 at 10-12 a.m. Rm. 69, 2nd floor

1 Confirmation of minutes

2 Matters arising from Oct. 25 meeting

3 Reports from task groups

4 Late items, AOB (any other business)

5 Closing

Minutes

Dear all

Below are the minutes from the April 1, 2010 board teleconference. Attendees: Sylvia, Udo, David and Chiara. Absent with regrets: John, Etsuko. Staff: Truus.

1 Approval of agenda as published: carried unanimously.

2 Motion F:04.10 to approve the Frankfurt bid for 2011

3 Date of next teleconference: May 10, 2010.

4 The meeting was adjourned at 5:30 p.m. EST.

Useful phrases

- Attached are the approved meeting minutes for the October annual meeting held October 2, 2009.
- Minutes of Berlin team meeting, 27th May 2009, 11-12.30 a.m., be approved and signed. (Noted)
- The next meeting for the London Project Management meeting will be on Fri. Nov. 13, 11 a.m,. in room 69-C.
- Could you please check the agenda, and be in touch with your questions and concerns? Thanks in advance.
- Attached is the report from our last meeting in Berlin, which was held on July 14. Should anyone miss anything, than please notify me before next Friday.
- It was decided to delay action until the next meeting.
- Please find below the agenda of ...
- The notes from the February 13 Business Unit meeting include ...
- Please take time to consider the minutes ...

Refusing a Request

The actual task of refusing someone something and yet maintaining goodwill is not the easiest one. But in the business world it simply does not suffice to refuse a request politely. There are methods however that will ensure that customers will want to continue doing business. Let us look at the four-step format below:

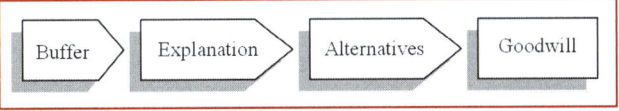

Checklist: negative messages

- **Buffer statement**: the first two sentences contain general neutral and positive remarks. They must be related to the refusal in the next paragraph.

- **Explanation**: in the second part of the e-mail explain why you cannot fulfil the request. Give logical reasons before you mention the negative message at the end of paragraph two. Also make sure the refusal is clear to avoid further debate on this topic.

- **Alternatives**: in the third paragraph try to demonstrate your concern for the reader. This way the reader also regains the psychological freedom after your refusal.

- **Goodwill ending**: which comes last is often remembered best. Therefore pay attention to a friendly ending.

Useful phrases

Buffer

- Thank you for bringing this matter to my attention.
- We regret to inform you that ...
- With regard to your request, unfortunately we are not able to ...

Explanation

- There appears to have been a misunderstanding.
- I have spoken to my line manager, and unfortunately we aren't able to …
- As we are bound by regulations of the …

Alternatives

- But I am sure we can find an acceptable compromise. I suggest you contact a@b.c to arrange this matter.
- We are however prepared to let you have the requested goods on credit.
- We could replace the damaged goods with …

Goodwill ending

- We offer you our sincere apologies for this.
- I have arranged for a member of our customer services team to give you a call later in the week.
- I very much hope you will continue to use our services in the future.

Stylistic stand back: negative – positive

Sometimes a negative phrase can sound much more positive by replacing the negative element which is in the word *not* by an alternative word. The table below gives some examples of this.

Implicitly negative	Explicitly negative
unable	not able
impossible	not possible
insignificant	not significant
irrelevant	not relevant
different	not the same
lacks	does not have
prevented	did not allow
unless	if ... not

Complaints

Complaints can be best dealt with in a neutral polite tone. To maintain a good working relationship, you might need to make a useful suggestion to solve the problem brought to your attention. Especially North American customers can be used to higher levels of personal service. In that sense a defensive approach might shut down effective communication. Providing rational explanations for a complaint probably gives better results.

Examples

Polite request

There seems to be an error in the invoice we received for goods delivered on May 22. As I discussed this morning with your associate Pete Johnsons, Muster GmbH notified you on May 16 of this matter.

May I ask you kindly to revise the billing statement by removing items ABC and sending us a cancelled invoice please? Thank you for your prompt attention to this matter.
Regards

Urgent
I am writing in connection with our order A-01, which arrived this morning. You sent us 11 ... instead of the 110 which we had ordered. This has caused us considerable difficulties, as our production unit needs the goods urgently. Unless we receive the goods by this Wednesday, we will have no choice but to cancel our order. I hope that ABC-AG will deal with this matter promptly.

Useful phrases

- We regret to write you that the products we received Friday, 13th were below the standard we expected.
- Please replace the broken goods as soon as possible.
- We wish to point out an error in the consignment we received yesterday.
- I hope that you will deal with this matter promptly, as it is causing us considerable inconvenience.

Apologies

When writing a formal e-mail to express regretful acknowledgement of a failure, you can choose from one of the alternatives listed below.

Useful phrases

Formal style

- I was very concerned to learn about your problems.
- We're doing everything we can to resolve this issue.
- Please accept our apologies for the inconvenience caused.
- This was due to circumstances beyond our control.
- I will look into the matter immediately and get back to you within the next few days.
- To compensate for the inconvenience caused by this, I would like to suggest ...
- We realise this is disappointing news to hear, and we apologise for the inconvenience we have caused you.
- We are sending you a ... as a gesture of goodwill ...

More personal style

- Please accept my sincere apologies for cancelling our appointment on such short notice.
- I had an unavoidable emergency that prevented me from keeping the appointment.
- An urgent matter at the head office came up that I just had to deal with immediately.
- On behalf of ABC GmbH, I offer sincere apologies to you for ...
- I'm afraid I had completely misunderstood the situation.
- The fault was entirely mine and I really regret that it occurred.

- I do hope we shall be able to put this unfortunate misunderstanding behind us.
- Once again, my sincere apologies.

Vocabulary:
inconvenience: Unbequemlichkeit
resolve: lösen, beikommen
circumstances: Umstände

Congratulations and Season's Greetings

In business, personal relationships will benefit from sending greetings on appropriate occasions.

Congratulations

- I was very happy to hear about your promotion to business unit manager. I congratulate you heartily.
- I would like to convey my sincere congratulations on winning the Prix de Rome.
- I am delighted to see that all your work has been recognised in this way.
- Please accept my warmest congratulations on your promotion to business unit manager.
- Once again my very best wishes.

Season's greetings

- We wish you a Merry Christmas and a happy New Year!
- Here is wishing you a happy holdiday season and all the best in the New Year.

Informal: congratulations

- Well done!
- I'm so glad to hear the news about ...
- Our sincere congratulations

Thanks

Formal style

- Our company is very grateful for the trouble you have taken to ...
- I'm writing to let you know how pleased Muster GmbH was with ...
- If the occasion arises, I hope you will allow us to return the favour.

More personal style

- I wanted to thank you again for such an enjoyable lunch yesterday.
- I am just writing to say what an excellent job you did of the Cologne project.
- Many thanks again for your help yesterday. If we can return the favour sometime, please let us know.

Short informal thanks

- Just a quick note to say many thanks for ...
- We really appreciate it.
- Thanks a lot / a million

Vocabulary:
convey: überbringen
favour: Gunst, Gefallen

Payments and Reminders

This paragraph is intended for anyone who is faced with the task of sending English e-mails in the financial world. Given the fact that some conventions are different (see the paragraph on numbers and currency symbols), it is good to know about such differences in advance.

Example

Dear Mr Holzbauer

We can confirm that we shipped your items, and that this completes your order. You can track the status of this order, online at: www.muster.de. Please note that tracking information may not be available immediately.

A copy of our invoice is attached as a PDF file. We kindly request you to remit the invoice amount within 14 days after invoice date.

Sincerely
Customer Service Department

Useful phrases

Sending invoices

- Please find enclosed a PDF copy of the invoice for our services.
- The total amount payable is: ...
- We request your remittance of the following balance by payment in advance: € 1,963.
- We request you to make remittance for the amount stated on the invoice to our account no later than 27 November 2009.
- We request you to make payment within 14 days to one of our accounts.
- We enclose a copy of our invoice for the goods delivered to you on ... against order number ...
- We ask you to settle the invoice by May 2.

Reminding payments

Intercultural text analyses have shown that differences exist between German and English in the way debt collection correspondence addresses readers. But although the tone might seem polite, the legal consequences are perfectly identical. Below are some useful phrases.

- We refer you to our conditions of payment.
- The outstanding invoices however must be paid by the end of this month.

- We should like to kindly remind you that our invoice no. 09-01 is due.
- In case you might have settled the account in the meantime, please ignore this e-mail.
- We kindly ask for early settlement of our invoice.
- We request payment of the invoice to account number ...
- We would be grateful if you could adjust the invoice accordingly.
- We have as yet had no reply to our request for payment.
- We must now insist on immediate payment.
- We need to take steps to collect the amount due.
- We hope you will understand our position.

Confirmations, inquiries and thanks

- We acknowledge receipt of the consignment.
- Could you please send us an amended invoice?
- At the current rate of exchange ...
- We have instructed our bank to pay you the sum owed.
- We have given instructions to our bank to make payment of € 1,963 against your invoice.
- We have transferred the sum of ... to your account.
- We thank you for your prompt payment of our invoice.

Useful vocabulary

bank connection	Bankverbindung
concerns	Betreff
BIC	BIC
date	Datum
foreign currency	Devisen, Fremdwährungen
total amount	Gesamtbetrag
fee	Honorar
IBAN	IBAN
bank account number	Kontonummer
Value Added Tax	Mehrwertsteuer
VAT	MwSt.
incidental expenses	Nebenkosten
invoice no.	Rechnungs- Nr.
amount of the invoice	Rechnungsbetrag
from	von
ATTN	z. Hd.
at the current rate of exchange	zum Tageskurs

Making Offers

Useful phrases

- We thank you for your enquiry about ...
- We are pleased to submit the following quotation ...
- We offer you the goods you specified as follows: ...
- Enclosed please find a sample of ...
- The prices are inclusive / exclusive of VAT.
- We can give you a discount of 13%.
- As long as supplies last.
- The offer/quotation excludes transportation costs.
- We hereby confirm your telephone order of ...
- This offer is non-binding and valid while supplies last.
- The goods will remain our legal property until full payment has been received.
- The prices and terms of delivery mentioned are binding until 27 November.
- Please refer to our conditions of sale for further particulars.
- You may rely on a quick and careful execution of your order.

Delivery and Incoterms

Useful phrases

- Delivery will be made immediately on receipt of your remittance.
- The goods will be transported by air.
- The merchandise is delivered ex factory (EXW).
- The consignment consists of: ...
- We take extra care in the packaging of our goods.
- We have booked your order and will do our best to carry out your request to your satisfaction.
- The products were sent to you today; the tracking number is: ...

Vocabulary:
remittance: Überweisung
consignment: Versand
tracking: Sendungsverfolgung

Incoterms

The Incoterms 2000 (International Commercial Terms: Internationale Regeln für die Auslegung von Handelsklauseln) are a series of international sales terms which serve to divide transaction costs and responsibilities between buyer and seller. They are usually mentioned in an abbreviation-city combination (e.g. our prices are FOB Hamburg).

Abbreviation	English	German
Group E		
EXW	Ex Works	Ab Werk
Group F		
FCA	Free Carrier	Frei Frachtführer
FAS	Free Alongside Ship	Frei Längsseite Schiff
FOB	Free On Board	Frei an Bord
Group C		
CFR	Cost and Freight	Kosten und Fracht
CIF	Cost, Insurance and Freight	Kosten, Versicherung, Fracht
CPT	Carriage Paid To	Frachtfrei
CIP	Carriage and Insurance Paid To	Frachtfrei versichert
Group D		
DAF	Delivered at Frontier	Geliefert Grenze
DES	Delivered Ex Ship	Geliefert ab Schiff
DEQ	Delivered Ex Quay	Geliefert ab Kai
DDU	Delivered Duty Unpaid	Geliefert unverzollt
DDP	Delivered Duty Paid	Geliefert verzollt

Numbers and Currency Symbols

When writing decimals or amounts of money, the English language observes a few other conventions compared to German.

- The most important difference probably is the reverse use of commas and full stops (periods):
  19,95 % (German) → 19.95% (English)
  16.090 km (German) → 10,000 miles (English)

- Amounts in round figures don't necessarily need a comma with two decimals behind it:
  25,00 EUR (German) → EUR 25 (English)

- The position of the currency can be placed before or behind the amount, depending on the local linguistic convention. There is no space between the pound sign and the amount in English.

- Another option is to use the ISO abbreviations for currencies in stead of the euro or pound sign. Notice the different position of the currency abbreviations:
  12.904,90 EUR (German) → GBP 10,000 (English)

- Please note that Australian texts may use a space instead of a comma, and Swiss texts often use an apostrophe to separate the thousands.

Indicating larger numbers

For describing larger amounts or numbers in the English language you may come across the following abbreviations:

- thousand: K
- million: M
- billion (*in German:* Milliarde): bn *or* B
- trillion (*in German:* Billion): T

Expressing numbers in alphabetic characters, such as *forty-three billion Canadian Dollars'*, finds application in official documents and in a formal or contractual context. But for sending e-mails around the globe, it's better to use figures.

Monetary and currency symbols

Monetary units, such as dollars or pound sterling, are often abbreviated with their own currency symbols. Note that in the United Kingdom a middle dot is often used as the decimal point on price stickers (e.g.: £6·95). Besides the currency symbols, you may also wish to write the international monetary abbreviations as stated in the list of currencies from the International Organization for Standardization (ISO 4217: Currency names and code elements).

List of currencies

Country	Currency	Sign	ISO	Fract.
Australia	Australian dollar	$	AUD	Cent
Bahamas	Bahamian dollar	$	BSD	Cent
Canada	Canadian dollar	$	CAD	Cent
Cyprus	Cypriot pound	£	CYP	Cent
Gibraltar	Gibraltar pound	£	GIP	Penny
Hong Kong	Hong Kong dollar	$	HKD	Ho
India	Indian rupee	₨	INR	Paisa
Ireland	Euro	€	EUR	Cent
Malaysia	Malaysian ringgit	RM	MYR	Sen
Malta	Maltese lira	₤	MTL	Cent
New Zealand	New Zealand dollar	$	NZD	Cent
Nigeria	Nigerian naira	₦	NGN	Kobo
Pakistan	Pakistani rupee	₨	PKR	Paisa
Singapore	Singapore dollar	$	SGD	Cent
South Africa	South African rand	R	ZAR	Cent
United Kingdom	British pound	£	GBP	Penny
United States	United States dollar	$	USD	Cent

Please note the differences in writing the word *euro*:

- The word *euro* is written in small letters in English.
- EU legislation prescribes using the words *euro* and *cent* both in singular and plural. But common usage in the rest of the English-speaking world is to use the natural plural in -s. Also most financial media in the UK prefer *euros* and *cents* as the plural forms.

Practical Reference

In this chapter you will find information on:

- linguistic characteristics as the use of capital letters or apostrophes and punctuation (page 86),

- linguistic Differences UK-USA (page 91),

- useful vocabulary and key terms for business correspondance (page 94),

- the use of abbreviations and acronyms etc. (page 99).

Linguistic Characteristics

The proper use of capital letters

In English the rules for using capitals are different from German rules.

Capital letters

In the following cases you do need to begin with capital letters:

- The pronoun 'I'
- Proper names
- Names of
  - the days of the week,
  - the months of the year,
  - holidays
  - historical periods
  - buildings
  - positions or titles of people
  - organisations
  - languages
  - nationalities or ethnic groups
- Words expressing a connection with geographical places
- Significant religious terms
- Roman numerals
- The first word of direct quotations, sentences or fragments

Small letters

Other elements are always written with small letters, such as:

- Names of directions (e.g.: south etc.)
- Names of seasons
- Articles in proper names (e.g.: the Emir of Kuwait)

The title or name of a book, a film or a magazine usually has capital letters for every significant word, but words like *the, of, and* or *in* aren't capitalized, unless they are the first word. Like in: *Yesterday we saw The Silence of the Lambs on TV.*

In British English the first word after a colon (double-point) generally is not written in capital letters. American usage on the other hand often prefers a capital after a colon. As mentioned above: with direct quotations both language varieties use a capital to start the quotation.

Vocabulary:
pronoun: (Personal)pronomen
numeral: Zahlwort
quotation: Zitat
proper name: Eigenname

Using apostrophes

The apostrophe (') is a troublesome punctuation mark in English, and incorrect use of apostrophes will make someone's writing quickly look poor. Still there is a lot of confusion about using apostrophes.

Contractions

The apostrophe is used in writing contractions, that is short-ened forms of words from which one or more letters have been omitted. The omitted letter is replaced by an apostrophe. Examples are: *it's* (*it is* or *it has*), *can't* (*cannot*), *aren't* (*are not*). When the word *not* is part of the contracted phrase, the apostrophe is always placed between the 'n' and the 't'. Traditionally contractions were considered as speaking language, and had no place whatsoever in formal business correspondence. Although using contractions in formal writing nowadays isn't considered wrong anymore, it's better to try to use them sparingly.

Full form	Contraction
cannot	can't
do not	don't
have not	haven't
he has (she)	he's, she's
he is (she)	he's, she's
I am	I'm
I have (we, you)	I've, we've, you've
I will / shall	I'll
is not	isn't
it has	it's
it is	it's
shall not	shan't
they are (we, you)	they're, we're, you're
will not	won't

Possessive forms

An apostrophe is also used in a possessive form like: *Hermann's report*. The basic rule is simple: a possessive form is spelled with 's' at the end. This also applies when the last letter is an 's', for instance like: *Klaus's proposal*. But there is an exception: plural nouns which already end in an 's', do not have a second 's'. They only have an apostrophe at the end as in: *four weeks' work*. When pluralising dates, there is a difference between British and American usage because the latter uses an apostrophe:

⬛ This model was designed in the 1990s.
⬛ This model was designed in the 1990's.

Using the spelling check

Especially in writing e-mails, spelling doesn't always seem to be a priority. Most errors can be simply prevented by using the spell check of your software. Below are some tips to make optimal use of this function. Always make sure that you turn on the function, and that you select the correct variety: for instance *English (United Kingdom)* or *English (United States)*. Besides local particular spelling conventions the second major difference is the vocabulary of each variety. The spell check takes this into account.

Homophones

One of the problems that German native speakers might have is that certain English words sound the same, but mean very different things, and they also don't have the same spelling.

The little poem below gives no indication whatsoever of a spell check, but is of course absolute nonsense.

> Finally eye used the English spelling chequer on my pea see,
> This marked four my revue, the miss steaks I could knot sea,
> So each time my chequer tolled me; eye quickly stroke the quay.

In linguistics these words are called homophones, i.e. words that have the same sound but a different spelling and meaning. Below is a selection of some relevant business homophones:

aisle	isle
buy	by
cell	sell
cent	scent
complement	compliment
fair	fare
hole	whole
hour	our
know	no
meat	meet
principal	principle
profit	prophet
right	write
sight	site
some	sum
stationary	stationery

Linguistic Differences: UK–USA

George Bernard Shaw once wrote that 'Britain and America are two countries divided by a common language'. But although there are some differences in spelling conventions or vocabulary, only a few words really cause misunderstandings. An example of this is the expression *to table a motion*. In the UK this means to place it on the agenda, while in the US it means exactly the opposite (to remove it from consideration). No idea how this is solved in bilateral meetings...

Spelling differences

If we take a closer look at the spelling differences between British and American English, the examples in the table below show you some typical spelling conventions. Many nouns and adjectives are turned into verbs by adding -ize (standardize) in the US, and -ise in Britain. If in doubt, you can simply adjust the spell check on your computer.

UK	US
authorise	authorize
litre, theatre, kilometre	liter, theater, kilometer
colour	color
catalogue	catalog
cheque	(bank) check
defence, offence	defense, offense
programme (except computer program)	program

UK	US
-our (labour, colour)	-or (labor, color)
-ogue (catalogue)	-og (catalog)
-ll (dialled, traveller)	-l (dialed, traveler)

But there are exceptions, for example: enrolment (UK), enrollment (US).

Different words

Besides the differences in spelling mentioned above, different words are simply used sometimes. Some of the more common ones are listed in the table below (listed by German translation for convenience):

Translation	UK	US
Bankkonto	banking account	bank account
Banknote	banknote	bill
Benzin	petrol	gas(oline)
Betrieb	company	corporation
Buchung	booking	reservation
Erkundigung	enquiry	inquiry
Führerschein	driving licence	driver's license
Herbst	autumn	fall
Lebenslauf	curriculum vitae	résumé, school transcript
Rechnung	bill	check
Rechtsanwalt	solicitor/barrister	attorney

Translation	UK	US
Reservierung	booking	reservation
Rückfahrkarte	return ticket	round trip ticket
Selbstkostenpreis	at cost price	at cost
Steuereinnahmen	inland revenue	duty income tax
Transport	transport	transportation
U-Bahn	underground	subway
Unterführung	subway	underpass
Verfallsdatum	expiry date	expiration date
vermieten	let	hire
vierzehn Tage	fortnight	two weeks
Wohnung	flat	apartment

Grammar differences

Some grammar differences are consistent between American and British:

UK	US
look out of the window	look out the window
last Monday week	a week ago last Monday
talk to, meet	talk with, meet with
I have (already) eaten	I (already) ate
River Thames, River Avon	Hudson River, Mississippi River
to be in a team	to be on a team
I've gone	I went

Apart from American and British, other well-known varieties of English are Canadian, Australian and South African. Countries such as India, Nigeria and the Philippines also have many English speakers.

Useful Vocabulary and Key Terms

Digital vocabulary

to	an
attachment	Anlage
@ (at sign)	At-Zeichen, Affenschwanz
subject	Betrifft, Betreff
hyphen	Bindestrich
file	Datei
e-mail	die E-Mail (D), das E-Mail (A, CH)
wireless	drahtlos
hard disk	Festplatte
to download	herunterladen
dot	Punkt
slash	Schrägstrich
back slash	umgekehrter Schrägstrich
underscore	Unterstrich
to forward	weiterleiten

Vocabulary: function keys

PgUp (page up)	Bild hoch
PgDn (page down)	Bild runter
PrtSc (Print Screen)	Druck
Insert	Einfg
End	Ende
Delete	Entf
Home	Post
Ctrl (control)	Strg
Shift	Ums

Key terms: e-mails

ASCII	American Standard Code for Information Interchange. A standard set of codes used for representing text and keyboard-control characters. Pronounced as: [aski]
Auto responder	A prewritten reply to an e-mail message, which is sent automatically
Bounced message	An e-mail that is returned to the sender because it cannot be delivered
Compression	File management technique that shrinks data for easy transportation. For instance: ZIP or RAR
Emoticons	Electronic symbols indicating emotions, e.g.: smileys
Encryption	Encoding or scrambling of an e-mail message or attachment for privacy reasons

Filter	A feature of an e-mail program to sort incoming messages
Flame	Angry or insulting e-mail messages
Forward	Retransmitting an e-mail message to other recipients
Group list	A group of e-mail addresses that can be addressed as a single recipient
Instant messaging (IM)	Direct exchange of messages with other people online
MIME	'Multipurpose Internet Mail Extensions': automatic recognition and display of file types
Priority	Designates an e-mail message's importance: high, normal or low priority
Signature	A personal identifier at the end of an e-mail message, informing on other contact data
Subject line	Topic of an e-mail message
Thread	An ongoing e-mail conversation
Word wrap	A feature in e-mail programs that allows insertion of soft returns at the right-side margins of an e-mail message

Key terms: the company

The following tables provide a quick reference source when trying to describe elements or divisions of a company.

Departments

orders	Bestellungen
accounting	Buchhaltung
purchasing	Einkauf
finance department	Finanzabteilung
research and development, R&D	Forschung und Entwicklung, F&E
information technology	IT-Abteilung
customer service	Kundenberatung
after-sales service	Kundenbetreuung
warehouse	Lagerhalle
logistics	Logistik
marketing	Marketing
assembly	Montage
public relations, PR	Öffentlichkeitsarbeit
human resources, personnel department	Personalabteilung
production	Produktion
legal department	Rechtsabteilung
sales department	Verkaufsabteilung
out-of-office sales	Verkaufs-Aussendienst
sales support	Verkaufs-Innendienst
sales management	Verkaufsleitung
despatch, dispatch	Versand
sales and distribution	Vertrieb
administration	Verwaltung
advertising department	Werbeabteilung

Company positions

shop floor worker	Arbeiter/-in
assistant	Assistent/-in
staff	Belegschaft
office staff	Büropersonal
director	Direktor, leitender Angestellter
managing director, CEO	Generaldirektor/-in
manager	Manager/-in
personnel	Personal
management	Unternehmensleitung
vice president	Vizepräsident/-in
supervisor	Vorgesetzter
chairman	Vorsitzender
board of managers	Vorstand

Company divisions

department, section	Abteilung
branch	Filiale, Niederlassung
business unit, division	Geschäftsbereich, Sparte
head office, head-quarters	Hauptsitz, Zentrale
holding company	Holdinggesellschaft
parent company	Muttergesellschaft
subsidiary	Tochtergesellschaft

Abbreviations and Acronyms

Because in e-mails people tend to write very quickly, many electronic acronyms have found their way into e-mail messages. In the table below you can find a selected overview of electronic acronyms and/or abbreviations that have found their way into business e-mail messages.

Only use abbreviations yourself if your readers (the intended as well as the hidden readers) will recognize and understand them. And don't use too many abbreviations, as they can make a sentence hard to read. Furthermore, it's advisable to clarify an uncommon abbreviation by writing it out on the first reference and citing the abbreviation in parentheses.

A/P	Accounts Payable
AA	Author's Alterations
abbr	Abbreviation, Abbreviated
abr	Abridged
abt	About
acc	According
acct	Account
acq	Acquired, Acquisition
ACWP	Actual Cost of Work Performed
Afaik	As Far As I Know
agg	Aggregated
AGM	Annual General Meeting
AKA	Also Known As
ANI	Automatic Number Identification

ans	Answer
apt	Apartment
ASAP	As Soon As Possible
ASL	Above Sea Level
ASP	Average Selling Price
ASR	Automatic Speech Recognition
asst	Assistant
AST	Atlantic Standard Time
Att	Attorney
Attn	Attention
Av	Avenue, Avenida
AWB	Air-Way Bill
AY	Academic Year
AYR	At Your Risk
B4	Before
BC	Before Christ
BE	Bill of Exchange
BKA	Better Known As
BL	Bill of Lading
bldg	Building
Bn	Billion
BP	Bill Payable
BPO	Business Process Outsourcing
BS	Bill of Sale
BSI	British Standards Institution

bsmt	Basement
BTW	By The Way
BW	Black and White
C&F	Cost And Freight
c/o	Care Of
c/w	Coming With
CAP	Customer Administration Panel
CBD	Cash Before Delivery
CBI	Confidential Business Information
CC	Carbon Copy, Customer Copy
CC	Chamber of Commerce
CCC	Customer Care Center
CDT	Central Daylight Time
CEO	Chief Executive Officer
CET	Central European Time, Centraal Eur.Tijd
CFO	Chief Financial Officer
CFP	Call For Proposals, Call For Papers
CFV	Call For Votes
ch	Chapter, Chapitre
chmn	Chairman
CIO	Chief Information Officer
cmte	Committee
Co	County
co	Care Of

Corp	Corporation
CPI	Consumer Price Index
CST	Central Standard Time
CT	Central Time
ctr	Center
DIY	Do It Yourself market
dna	Does Not Apply
DoB	Date Of Birth
e.g.	Exempli Gratia
EDT	Eastern Daylight Time
Esq	Esquire
EST	Eastern Standard Time
ewt	Elsewhere Taken
F	Floor
F2F	Face to Face
FAO	For the Attention Off
FAQ	Frequently Asked Question(s)
ff	Following
FMCG	Fast-Moving Consumer Goods
FOB	Free on Board
FSS	Financial Services Sector
FTC	Free Trade Committee
FY	Fiscal Year
FYI	For Your Information
GA	General Average

GL	Ground Level
GMT	Greenwich Mean Time
H&S	Health And Safety
HR	Human Resource
i.e.	Id Est
i/c	In Charge
ICT	Information & Communication Technology
Imho	In My Humble Opinion
imo	In My Opinion
IOW	In Other Words
ITT	Invitation To Tender
JIT	Just In Time
KISS	Keep It Short and Simple
L/C	Letter of Credit
LL	Lines
M/F	Male or Female
MD	Managing Director
mfg	Manufacturing
misc	Miscellaneous
MoM	Minutes Of Meeting
mph	Miles Per Hour
MSGS	Messages
n/a	Not Applicable
NB	Nota bene

NDA	Non-Disclosure Agreement
NLT	No Later Than
NOTA	None Of The Above
o/a	On Account
PA	Personal Assistant
pct	Percent, Procent
pkwy	Parkway
PLS	Please
PM	Post Meridiem, Past Mid-day
PM	Prime Minister
pp	Pages
PPI	Producers Price Index
PS	Pound Sterling
PT	Part-Time
PTO	Patent and Trademark Office
Pty	Property, Proprietary
REC'D	Received
RGDS	Regards
RoI	Return On Investment
SMB	Small or Medium Business
SME	Small and Medium-sized Enterprises
SOHO	Small Office, Home Office
Spec	Specification
SSN	Social Security Number
T/B	Top and Bottom

TBC	To Be Considered
THX	Thanks
TIA	Thanks In Advance
TS/SI	Top Secret/Sensitive Information
TWIC	To Whom It Concerns
USASI	USA Standards Institute
USPTO	United States Patent and Trademark Office
VSB	Very Small Business
w/	With
w/o	Without
WRT	With Regards To

A special e-mail style

Besides such expressions another form of abbreviated words in e-mail developed. In this style, the vowels are often deleted, or parts of words are replaced by homonyms:

Subject: Thx for yr msg
Re your msg on our ans machine: gr8 you've got a back-up :-)
Hv 2 work now. CU,
Silke

Although you may occasionally come across this kind of new abbreviation, it is nevertheless discouraged from using them in formal business correspondence.

Full stops or periods?

There is a tendency in Great-Britain to write abbreviations without a full stop (period). British usage favours omitting the full stop in abbreviations which include the first and last letters of a single word, such as *Mr, Mrs, Ms, Dr* or *St* – American usage on the contrary prefers: *Mr., Mrs., Ms., Dr. and St.*, with full stops. Two other common abbreviations are *a.m.* and *p.m.*, like in: *11.00 a.m.* or *five p.m.* Note that these are not capitalised in British usage. Funnily enough American usage here prefers capitals and no full stops, so *11:00 AM* or *five PM.*

False Friends

False friends (or faux amis) are pairs of words that look similar, but differ in meaning in two languages. As false friends are a problem for second language speakers, the table below simultaneously compiles some common German-English as well as English-German false friends.

German	English	False friend	Translation
auch	also	also	thus, therefore
Bedeutung	meaning	Meinung	opinion
bekommen	to get	to become	werden
Direktion	management	direction	Richtung
eigentlich	actual(ly)	aktuell	up-to-date
ich werde	I will	Ich will	I want to
Konkurrenz	competition	concurrence	Einverständnis

German	English	False friend	Translation
Konzept	draft, plan	concept	Begriff, Idee
Konzern	corporate	concern	Belang
Manager	CEO	manager	Filialleiter
Marke	brand	mark	Note
Messe	fair, mass	mess	Unordnung
Personal	personnel	personal	persönlich
schließlich	eventually	eventuell	possibly
schnell	fast	fast	almost
Streit	argument	Argument	point
Unternehmer	entrepreneur	undertaker	Leichen-bestatter
wenn	if	when	wann
werden	to become	bekommen	to receive

E-mail Features

Formatting e-mail for foreign screens

A common problem is the way e-mails look on the screen of the receiver. I tested this once by sending an e-mail to five different people, whom I asked to print and fax the message to me. Not one of them looked like the original. Some of the main differences that appeared: specific German letters (ß, Ü, Ä, etc.) were replaced by strings of other characters; Internet addresses no longer worked like hyperlinks; italicised letters didn't show; word wrap influenced the look and feel of the text. The average line length is 75 characters (screen width).

To avoid such discordances in international business you could use the following techniques:

- In your options you can choose 'MIME encoding', instead of 'BinHex' or 'Uuencode'. In the 'Options window' you can also set lines to wrap automatically at 65 to 75 characters.

- Probably it's best to choose 'plain text' (also known as ASCII) in stead of 'HTML' in the settings of your e-mail program. Then once you know that the addressee's software is capable of interpreting all symbol codes correctly, you can always opt for fancier settings. One problem with ASCII however, is that the only characters that are sure to be properly transmitted are those with ASCII/ANSI numbers between 32 and 126. Thus, an outgoing German character (usually falling outside the range 32-126) transmitted from a German QWERTZ keyboard is likely to be converted into something else. To be on the safe side you can replace the following typical characters with alternative keyboard combinations.

Character	Alternative	Majuskel	Minuskel
Ä	ae	Alt-142	Alt-132
Ö	oe	Alt-153	Alt-148
Ü	ue	Alt-154	Alt-129
ß	ss	Alt-225	Alt-225

- Another point is the downloading of images that are connected to the content. It might look great before sending, but many people have set their mail software to block automatic picture downloads and other external content in messages (if the content is linked to a server). In the recipient's inbox this results in sloppy areas showing messages that the content needs to be downloaded first. Not necessarily the best first impression.

Templates

Form letters or templates are reusable letter elements. They were invented for a reason, namely because they can save people a lot of time if used properly. In certain jobs people probably need to write the same type of e-mail over and over again, as both purpose and content are essentially the same. The following situations lend themselves to templates:

- Meeting announcements, agendas and minutes,
- Common requests and responses to common questions,
- Sales letters or other marketing messages.
- Regular reports and project updates

In the example below you can see a typical message that is qualified for a template. The fields between square brackets can be typed in manually, but also be connected to an excel spreadsheet (containing product or address information e.g.).

Example

This is a reminder of the weekly meeting: [date, time and loca-tion].

May I ask you to please send me any additions and/or correc-tions at least two days before the meeting.

Also, please let me know if you won't be able to attend.

Thanks,
Aynur

Checklist: using e-mail templates

- First analyse your existing e-mails or responses to see what the essential elements are.

- Keep the template files up-to-date over the years.

- Besides features like 'Autotext' there are also specific (free) software programs available on Internet to help you streamline the writing process.

- Try to make a habit of always proofreading the mails you create from templates before sending them out.

Identifying international e-mails

People who are used to electronic addresses ending with dot-de or dot-com might have some difficulties with the type of addresses that use a second level domain (SLD). Usu-ally such extra codes indicate an activity (*co* for companies, *gov* for governments, etc.). Such an address contains an extra dot and the specific code, e.g.: www.bbc.co.uk. In fact, quite a number of countries use this type of electronic address. In addition to most Commonwealth countries and South America, countries like Austria, Sweden, Turkey or Japan, also use such URLs.

When trying to locate a website it can be practical to know the suffix of the country in question. The list below gives an overview for Anglophone countries.

Code	English	German
sld*.au	Australia	Australien
.ca	Canada	Kanada
sld.hk	Hong Kong	Hongkong
sld.in	India	Indien
.ie	Ireland	Irland
sld.nz	New Zealand	Neuseeland
sld.za	South Africa	Südafrika
sld.uk	United Kingdom	Großbritannien
.com, .gov *etc.*	United States	Vereinigte Staaten

* *sld.* means *second level domain*, e.g.: www.airberlin.co.uk

Legal implications of e-mail

The first publicised case, in which an e-mail was used as evidence, was the Iran-Contra scandal, which involved the White House and Lt. Col. Oliver North. In the past few years, e-mails have often made the news headlines. The lesson learned is that e-mails, written in a certain way, can result in companies being confronted with legal liability. This can happen in three ways basically:

- When the content of the mail involves exaggerations, guarantees, leaking of sensitive information and/or the spreading of rumours.

- People can be presumed to have knowledge of the contents of an e-mail once it arrived on their workstation. E-mail can create a responsibility to report in this way.

- Forwarding electronic clippings in an e-mail implies a possible violation of copyright laws.

Vocabulary:
liability: Haftung
presume: annehmen
violation: Übertretung, Verletzung

Responding to e-mail

Recent surveys reveal that we now spend between 30 minutes and four hours or more a day on e-mail-related activities. What tactics can you use to manage the e-mail interruptions? If you compare e-mail to let's say phone calls, then why do we use our precious times replying to certain information? I ask this because on the phone you probably wouldn't respond. However, quite a few people can click on the reply button probably faster than they can pronounce the word *reply*. And they do so despite the fact that many of these messages may need no response at all. Therefore, when a sender is only passing along information and has not asked for a reply, probably just reading, filing or deleting the e-mail suffices.

Quite often it's possible to summarise the key points or questions from several individual messages. Combine your responses into one e-mail that includes answers to questions, provides the necessary details, and so on. Also don't open e-mails you don't really need to read.

Checklist: responding to e-mail

By using the questions below you can see whether you respond appropriately and efficiently to the e-mails you receive.

- Wouldn't it be quicker to reply on the phone or in person than in an e-mail?

- Is a response really necessary? Or can you just file, print out, forward or delete the e-mail?

- Do you need some time to think or calm down first? In this case, don't respond immediately.

- Do you need to inform others by Cc or Bcc?

- In case you decide to copy people, do they really need to have that information, and will they think of it as useful?

- Did you run a spell check?

- Is it necessary for you to respond at this very moment?

Tables and Overviews

Types of companies

In many e-mail signatures businesses will write a company name with suffixes like AG, GmbH etc. This paragraph gives an overview of the different abbreviations that are in use in the Anglophone world. Although the judicial systems are very different, it is still sometimes very handy to have some kind of comparison. Therefore a German equivalent has been added, if applicable.

Abbr.	Country	Legal entity	Equivalent
Assocs.	USA	Associates	
(Edms.) Bpk.	RSA	Proprietary Limited (Afrikaans: Beperk)	GmbH
CC / BK	RSA	Close Corporation (Afrikaans: Beslote Korporasie)	
	UK	Company Limited by Guarantee	
	UK	Sole proprietorship, one-man business	EU
	UK	Unlimited Company	GmbH
Co.	USA	Company	
Corp.	USA	Corporation (see: Incorporated)	AG
Cpt	Irl	Cuideachta phoiblé theoranta (Public Limited Company)	AG
d/b/a	USA	Doing Business As.	EU

Abbr.	Country	Legal entity	Equivalent
ELP	Bah	Exempted Limited Partnership.	
IBC	Bah	International Business Company	offshore
Inc.	Can	Incorporated. Limited Liability	
Inc.	Aus	Incorporated Association	
Inc.	USA	Incorporated	AG
L.P.	USA	Limited Partnership	
LLC	USA	Limited Liability Company	
LLP	USA	Limited Liability Partnership	
LTD	Aus, India	Limited	GmbH
Ltd.	Can	Limited (Quebec: Limitée, Ltée)	GmbH
Ltd.	NZ, RSA	Limited	GmbH
Ltd.	UK	Private Limited Company	GmbH
(Pty.) Ltd.	RSA	Proprietary Limited	GmbH
N.A.	USA	National Association	für Banken
NT	Can	Intermediary	
P.C.	USA	Professional Corporation	
P/L or Pty. Ltd.	Aus	Proprietary Limited Company.	GmbH
PC Ltd	Aus	Public Company Limited by Shares	

Abbr.	Country	Legal entity	Equivalent
PLC	Irl	Public Limited Company	AG
PLC	UK	Public Limited Company	AG
PrC	Irl	Private Company Limited by Shares	GmbH
Pty.Ltd. Pte.Ltd.	Various	Proprietary Limited company	GmbH
Pvt. Ltd.	India	Private Limited Company	GmbH
Teo	Irl	Teoranta	GmbH

Country abbreviations

Aus: Australia; Bah: Bahamas; Can: Canada; Irl: Irland; NZ: New Zealand; RSA: South Africa; UK: Großbritannien; USA: Vereinigte Staaten.

German abbreviations

AG: Aktiengesellschaft; GmbH: Gesellschaft mit beschränkter Haftung; EU: Einzelunternehmen.

Official holidays and translations

Finding the right translation for a national holiday during a conversation can be difficult. How would you explain *Mariä Himmelfahrt* or *Pfingsten* in English? Below are English-German translations for the most commonly celebrated official holidays. Their specific dates can be found in the next paragraph:

Holiday	Translation
New Year's Day	Neujahr
Epiphany	Heilige Drei Könige
Carnival	Karneval / Fasching
Good Friday	Karfreitag
Easter	Ostern
Labour Day	Tag der Arbeit
Ascension Day	Christi Himmelfahrt
Whit Sunday	Pfingsten (Pfingstsonntag)
Whit Monday	Pfingstmontag
Corpus Christi	Fronleichnam
Midsummer's Day	Johannistag / Sommersonnen-wende
Assumption	Mariä Himmelfahrt
All Saints' Day	Allerheiligen
Christmas Eve	Heiligabend
Christmas Day	Erster Weihnachtsfeiertag
Boxing Day	Zweiter Weihnachtsfeiertag
New Year's Eve	Silvester
National Day	Nationalfeiertag (auch für: Tag der deutschen Einheit)
Liberation Day	Tag der Befreiung

What are bank holidays?

A bank holiday is a public holiday in the United Kingdom and in the Republic of Ireland. Bank holidays are so called because they are the days upon which banks were closed by tradition (since the Bank Holidays Act of 1871). England and Wales share the same days, but Scotland, Northern Ireland and the Republic of Ireland all have their own public holiday.

Country-specific holidays

Besides the commonly celebrated holidays, most countries have specific local public holidays.

Australia

26 January - Australia Day, 25 April - ANZAC Day, second Monday in June - Queen's birthday

Canada

24 May - Victoria Day, 1 July - Canada Day, first Monday in September - Labour Day, second Monday in October - Thanksgiving, 11 November - Remembrance Day

England and Wales

7 May - May Day Bank Holiday, 28 May - Spring Bank Holiday, 27 August - Summer Bank Holiday

Ireland

St. Patrick's Day, first Monday in May, June, August last Monday in October

New Zealand

6 February - Waitangi Day, 25 April - ANZAC Day, first Monday in June - Queen's birthday, fourth Monday in October - Labour Day

Northern Ireland

17 March - St Patrick's Day, 7 May - May Day Bank Holiday, 28 May - Spring Bank Holiday, 12 July - Orangeman's Day, 27 August - Summer Bank Holiday

Scotland

2 January - 2 January, 7 May - May Day Bank Holiday, 28 May - Spring Bank Holiday, 6 August - Summer Bank Holiday, 30 November - St. Andrew's Day

South Africa

21 March - Human Rights Day, 27 April - Freedom Day, 1 May - Workers' Day, 16 June - Youth Day, 9 August - National Women's Day, 24 September - Heritage Day, 16 December - Day of Reconciliation

United States

Traditionally 30 May - Memorial Day, first Monday in September - Labor Day, 4 July - Independence Day - 4th Thursday in November - Thanksgiving Day

Translated geographical names

A number of cities in German-speaking regions have different names in English. The list below helps to prevent misunderstandings when giving address information.

Bayern	Bavaria
Braunschweig	Brunswick
Franken	Franconia
Frankfurt am Main	Frankfort
Hannover	Hanover
Koblenz	Coblenz
Köln	Cologne
Luzern	Lucerne
München	Munich
Niedersachsen	Lower Saxony
Nordrhein	Westfalen
North Rhine	Westphalia
Nürnberg	Nuremberg
Preußen	Prussia
Rheinland Pfalz	Rhineland Palatinate
Ruhrgebiet	Ruhr River Valley
Sachsen	Saxony
Schwaben	Swabia
Steiermark	Styria
Thüringen	Thuringia
Tirol	Tyrol
Westfalen	Westphalia
Wien	Vienna

Temperature conversion table

Fahrenheit (°F)	Celsius (°C)
212 (boiling point)	100 (Siedepunkt)
176	80
122	50
104	40
98.4 (body temperature)	37 (Körpertemperatur)
68	20
50	10
32 (freezing point)	0 (Gefrierpunkt)
14	-10
0	-17,8
-459.67 (absolute zero)	-273,15 (absoluter Nullpunkt)

Conversion of Celsius and Fahrenheit:

- °F - °C: (°F - 32) x 5/9 = °C
- °C - °F: °C x 9/5 + 32 = °F

Weights and measures

Weights	Gewichte
gross weight	Bruttogewicht
net weight	Nettogewicht
1 ounce (oz)	28,35 g
1 pound (lb)	453,6 g
1 stone	6,356 kg
1 short hundredweight (cwt)	45,359 kg (USA)
1 long hundredweight (cwt)	50,802 kg (GB)
1 short ton (tn)	907 kg (USA)
1 long ton (tn)	1016 kg (GB)
1 metric ton	1000 kg
Linear measures	Längenmaße
1 inch (in)	2,54 cm
1 foot (ft)	30,48 cm (12 in)
1 yard (yd)	91,44 cm (3 ft)
1 mile (m)	1,609 km (1760 yd)

Electronic Guidelines on Internet

- Paradigm Online Writing Assistant:
  www.powa.org

- Regeln und Schreibweisen der Europäischen Union:
  http://publications.europa.eu/code/de/de-000100.htm

- BBC Style guide:
  www.bbctraining.com/pdfs/newsStyleGuide.pdf

- Deutsch-Englisches Wörterbuch:
  http://dict.leo.org

Index

Bibliografische Information der Deutschen Bibliothek
Die Deutsche Bibliothek verzeichnet diese Publikation in der Deutschen Nationalbiblio-
grafie; detaillierte bibliografische Daten sind im Internet über http://dnb.ddb.de
abrufbar.

ISBN 978-3-448-08815-1
Bestell-Nr. 00975-0001

© 2009, Rudolf Haufe Verlag GmbH & Co. KG, Niederlassung Planegg /München
Postanschrift: Postfach, 82142 Planegg
Hausanschrift: Fraunhoferstraße 5, 82152 Planegg
Fon (0 89) 8 95 17-0, Fax (0 89) 8 95 17-2 50
E-Mail: online@haufe.de
Internet: www.haufe.de
Redaktion: Jürgen Fischer
Redaktionsassistenz: Christine Rüber

Gesamtbetreuung und Lektorat: Sylvia Rein, 81371 München
Umschlaggestaltung: Simone Kienle, 70182 Stuttgart
Umschlagentwurf: Agentur Buttgereit & Heidenreich, 45721 Haltern am See

Druck: freiburger graphische betriebe, 79108 Freiburg

Der Autor

Sander Schroevers

arbeitet in den Niederlanden, Frankreich und Deutschland als Berater im Bereich der internationalen Kommunikation und PR. Er spricht häufig auf internationalen Konferenzen und hat bereits zahlreiche Bücher auf dem Feld der europäischen Kommunikation publiziert. Daneben ist er Präsident des IECIE-Gremiums, dem Europäischen Institut für Internationale Unternehmenskommunikation (l'institut européen de communication internationale d'entreprise) in Paris, Frankreich.

Internet: www.schroevers.eu

Weitere Literatur

„Phone Calls in English", von Sander M. Schroevers, 128 Seiten, € 6,90, ISBN 978-3-448-08627-0, Bestell-Nr. 00967

„Business Talk English", von Stuart Dean, 128 Seiten, € 6,90, ISBN 978-3-448-08623-2, Bestell-Nr. 00962

„Presentations in English", von Jaquie Mary Thomas, 128 Seiten, € 6,90, ISBN 978-3-448-08734-5 Bestell-Nr. 00972

„Business Knigge international" von Kai Oppel, 192 Seiten, € 19,80, ISBN 978-3-448-08747-5, Bestell-Nr. 00076

TaschenGuides – Qualität entscheidet